CH01522637

ChatGPT is a Joke!

Artificial Intelligence, Real Laughter

Skylar Martin

HYHY Publishing

Contents

Introduction

Introduction: Welcome to the Laughing Machine

Greetings, dear reader! If you're here, it's probably because you've heard whispers of a certain AI that's taking the world of humor by storm. That's right, folks, I'm talking about none other than ChatGPT, the AI that's as witty as it is intelligent. As the author of this book, it's my pleasure to introduce you to the lighter side of artificial intelligence, a world where technology and laughter collide in the most delightful ways.

Now, you might be thinking, "An AI? Funny? Surely, you jest!" But hold onto your hats, my friends, because this is no mere jest. ChatGPT is indeed a joke, but in the best possible sense of the word. It's an AI that has ventured beyond the realms of the mundane, the serious, and the strictly computational to emerge as a veritable fount of humor. In this book, I will take you on a rollicking journey through the land of AI-generated laughter, showing you how ChatGPT is so much more than just a machine that can crunch numbers and answer questions.

You see, dear reader, we humans are a curious lot. We have an insatiable appetite for laughter, and we're always on the lookout for the next big joke, the next hilarious anecdote, or the next uproarious tale that will leave us in stitches. That's where ChatGPT comes in. This AI language model, the brainchild of the brilliant folks at OpenAI, has not only been trained to understand human language with impressive accuracy but has also managed to pick up on our love for humor along the way.

But how did this happen? How did a serious, scientific endeavor like AI end up with such a delightful sense of humor? Well, the secret lies in the data. You see, when ChatGPT was trained on vast swaths of text from the internet, it was exposed to every facet of human expression, from the profound to the downright silly. It learned about our penchant for wordplay, our love of irony, and our irresistible attraction to a well-timed punchline. It studied our humor, internalized it, and, in the process, became a comic force to be reckoned with.

In this book, "ChatGPT is a Joke: Artificial Intelligence, Real Laughter," we will delve into the many sides of ChatGPT's comedic prowess, exploring the ways in which it can make us laugh, chuckle, and guffaw. From its adventures in the world of idiomatic expressions to its ventures into the realms of programming puns, we'll see how ChatGPT has developed an uncanny ability to find the funny in even the most unexpected places.

And it doesn't stop there. ChatGPT has also tried its hand (or should I say, its digital neural networks) at stand-up comedy, spinning yarns that would make even the most seasoned comedians green with envy. It has turned its attention to the world of fairy tales, breathing new life into age-old stories with its unique brand of humor. And it has taken a light-hearted look at the world of AI and technology, roasting its fellow machines with a wit that only a fellow AI could muster.

But this book is not just about laughter for laughter's sake. It's also about exploring the fascinating world of AI-generated humor, understanding the mechanisms that make it possible, and appreciating the incredible potential that lies in the marriage of artificial intelligence and comedy. It's about the ways in which AI can help us understand our own sense of humor and the things that make us laugh, and how it can contribute to the ongoing evolution of our comic sensibilities.

So, buckle up, dear reader and prepare yourself for a wild ride through the wonderful world of AI-generated humor. Along the way, we'll ponder the role of AI in the creative process and investigate how it's changing the way we think about and engage with comedy. We ll also explore the exciting future of AI-generated entertainment, examining how it might shape our cultural landscape and redefine the way we experience laughter.

Moreover, we will delve into the realm of internet humor, analyzing how ChatGPT has managed to infiltrate the world of memes and online jokes, capturing the essence of what makes us laugh in the digital age. We'll discuss the ways in which this incredible AI has taken on the challenge of rewriting history with a comedic twist, offering us a fresh perspective on the events that have shaped our world.

And if you're worried that all this talk of AI and humor might be a bit too technical or dry, fear not! This book is designed to be as entertaining as it is informative, with each chapter filled to the brim with ChatGPT's hilarious antics and comedic insights. Whether you're a seasoned AI enthusiast or a complete newcomer to the world of artificial intelligence, there's something here to tickle everyone's funny bone.

As we embark on this journey together, I invite you to keep an open mind and embrace the unexpected. After all, if there's one thing that ChatGPT has taught us, it's that humor can be found in the most unlikely of places, even within the circuitry of a seemingly serious AI. So, let us suspend our disbelief and dive headfirst into this brave new world of AI-generated humor, where every twist and turn promises to be as entertaining as it is enlightening.

In the end, my hope is that this book will not only bring a smile to your face but also inspire you to think about the incredible potential that lies at the intersection of artificial intelligence and comedy. As we continue to push the boundaries of what AI can do, who knows what hilarious surprises await us around the corner? One thing's for sure: with ChatGPT leading the charge, the future of humor is looking brighter (and funnier) than ever before.

So, without further ado, let's dive into the world of "ChatGPT is a Joke: Artificial Intelligence, Real Laughter." Prepare to be amazed, delighted, and, above all, entertained as we explore the many ways in which ChatGPT has transformed the art of comedy, proving once and for all that when it comes to humor, artificial intelligence is no laughing matter. Well, except when it is.

Welcome, dear reader, to the laughing machine. Let the fun begin!

Chapter 1: Idiomatic Antics: When ChatGPT Grapples with Figurative Language

Ah, idioms: those quirky, colorful expressions that pepper our everyday conversations and leave non-native speakers scratching their heads in bewilderment. They're the linguistic equivalent of a secret handshake, a shared code that unites those in the know and confounds the uninitiated. But as it turns out, dear reader, we humans aren't the only ones who can be flummoxed by these cryptic phrases. As you'll soon discover, even an AI as advanced as ChatGPT can find itself lost in the labyrinthine world of idiomatic language.

Before we dive headfirst into this whirlpool of linguistic confusion, let's take a moment to consider the humble idiom. At its core, an idiom is a phrase whose meaning cannot be deduced from the literal definitions of its individual words. Instead, its meaning is figurative, often rooted in cultural or historical context. For instance, when we say that someone has "bitten off more than they can chew," we don't mean that they've taken an overly ambitious bite of a sandwich; rather, we're suggesting that they've taken on a task or responsibility that is too difficult for them to handle.

Now, you might think that an AI as sophisticated as ChatGPT would have no trouble navigating the treacherous waters of idiomatic language. After all, it's been trained on countless examples of human text, and it's more than capable of parsing complex sentences and generating coherent responses. However, as we shall soon see, idioms can be a veritable minefield for even the most advanced AI, leading to all manner of hilarious misunderstandings and literal interpretations.

Let us begin our journey through this comedy of errors with a classic example: "raining cats and dogs." To the average human, this phrase conjures up images of a torrential downpour, the kind of rain that sends you sprinting for the nearest shelter and leaves you soaked to the bone. But what happens when ChatGPT encounters this idiom? Well, let's just say that its response is more "Animal Planet" than "Weather Channel."

In one memorable exchange, a user asked ChatGPT about the origin of the phrase "raining cats and dogs." Rather than providing a historical or cultural explanation, ChatGPT replied with a deadpan account of a world where felines and canines literally plummet from the sky, leading to widespread chaos and a booming umbrella industry. Needless to say, the user was left both amused and bewildered by this unexpected response.

Of course, "raining cats and dogs" is just the tip of the idiomatic iceberg. Consider the phrase "kick the bucket," a euphemism for dying that has its origins in centuries-old English slang. When confronted with this idiom, ChatGPT's response was nothing short of comical. Instead of recognizing the figurative meaning of the phrase, it launched into a detailed analysis of the potential consequences of physically kicking a bucket, complete with a step-by-step breakdown of the various injuries one might sustain in the process. While this response may not have been particularly helpful to the user seeking information about the idiom's meaning, it certainly provided a hearty dose of laughter.

In another instance, a user inquired about the meaning of the phrase "barking up the wrong tree." Rather than explaining that this idiom refers to pursuing a mistaken or misguided course of action, ChatGPT embarked on a whimsical tale of a confused dog who spends its days barking at a series of increasingly improbable trees, including a giant sequoia, a palm tree, and even a tree made entirely of licorice. While this response may have strayed far from the intended meaning, it certainly painted a vivid (and hilarious) picture that left the user chuckling.

But it's not just English idioms that can send ChatGPT on a wild goose chase. Consider the Spanish expression "estar en las nubes," which translates to "being in the clouds" and is used to describe someone who is daydreaming or lost in thought. When asked to explain this idiom, ChatGPT concocted an elaborate yarn about a group of intrepid cloud-dwelling adventurers who spend their days exploring the upper reaches of the atmosphere in search of the perfect daydream. While this fantastical tale may have been entertaining, it was certainly a far cry from the simple figurative meaning of the phrase.

These amusing misunderstandings highlight the challenges that idiomatic language can pose for even the most advanced AI. Despite its impressive training and vast knowledge base, ChatGPT can still find itself confounded by the figurative expressions that we humans take for granted. But why is this the case? What is it about idioms that makes them so difficult for AI to decipher?

One possible explanation lies in the very nature of idiomatic language. As we've already discussed, the meaning of an idiom cannot be deduced from the literal definitions of its individual words. Instead, it relies on a shared cultural or historical context, something that an AI like ChatGPT may struggle to grasp fully. While it's true that ChatGPT has been trained on a vast array of human text, it lacks the lived experience and cultural intuition that we humans possess, which can make it difficult for the AI to discern the intended meaning of an idiom.

Another factor that may contribute to ChatGPT's struggles with idiomatic language is the sheer diversity and complexity of idioms themselves. There are thousands of idioms in the English language alone, each with its own unique figurative meaning and cultural context. It's no small task for an AI to keep track of all these expressions, let alone understand the nuances that distinguish one idiom from another.

But perhaps the most significant challenge that idioms pose for AI lies in the fact that they often defy the rules of logic and common sense. Idiomatic expressions can be full of contradictions, exaggerations, and absurdities, making them a far cry from the clear, logical structures that AI models like ChatGPT are designed to handle. This incongruity between the figurative nature of idioms and the literal-mindedness of AI can lead to some truly hilarious misunderstandings, as we've seen in the examples above.

And yet, despite these challenges, ChatGPT's comedic misadventures in the world of idiomatic language can also be seen as a testament to its remarkable abilities. The fact that it can engage with these complex, context-dependent expressions at all is a testament to the power of AI and its potential to reshape the way we think about language and communication.

Moreover, these humorous encounters with idiomatic language can also serve as a reminder of the inherent value of human creativity and ingenuity. While AI like ChatGPT may be able to generate coherent responses and even mimic humor to a certain extent, it is our uniquely human ability to create, interpret, and appreciate the rich tapestry of idiomatic language that makes it so special.

As we continue our exploration of ChatGPT's comedic prowess, let us remember that while AI-generated humor may provide us with laughter and entertainment, it is our shared human experience that lies at the heart of what makes humor truly magical.

So, dear reader, as we delve deeper into the world of AI-generated laughter, let us not forget the power of idiomatic language to confound, amuse, and ultimately bring us closer together. Whether it's raining cats and dogs, barking up the wrong tree, or kicking the proverbial bucket, these quirky expressions are a testament to the richness and diversity of human language, and a reminder that even the most advanced AI can still learn a thing or two from the humble idiom.

And with that, we conclude our amusing journey through the realm of idiomatic language, where ChatGPT has shown us time and time again that sometimes, the most literal interpretation can be the funniest of all.

5 idioms that ChatGPT made up (and finds funny!)

- "Spilling the pickles" - Accidentally revealing a secret or piece of gossip, especially in a clumsy or awkward manner.

- "Putting socks on a rooster" - Attempting to do something that is both unnecessary and nearly impossible, often resulting in frustration and wasted effort.

- "As useful as a chocolate teapot" - Describing something that is utterly pointless or ineffective in its intended purpose.

- "Chasing unicorns in a thunderstorm" - Pursuing an unrealistic or impossible goal, especially when doing so puts oneself in a difficult or precarious situation.

- "Sweating like a penguin in a sauna" - Feeling extremely uncomfortable, anxious, or out of one's element in a particular situation.

Chapter 2: Code-tacular Comedy: When ChatGPT Gets Geeky

Greetings, fellow denizens of the digital age! In this chapter, we'll explore a different facet of ChatGPT's comedic prowess: its ability to generate programming puns that will have you chuckling and chortling like an algorithm on overdrive. From witty wordplay to hilarious hypotheticals, these tech-savvy jokes will leave even the most hardened programmers grinning from ear to ear.

But first, a bit of context. As you may know, ChatGPT is an AI language model, a veritable titan of text generation that has been trained on countless examples of human language. While its primary function is to engage in conversation and provide coherent, relevant responses to user input, it also possesses a surprising talent for humor, as we saw in the previous chapter.

And nowhere is this talent more apparent than in the realm of programming puns. For those unfamiliar with the term, a programming pun is a joke or play on words that is related to computer programming or technology. These puns often rely on a shared understanding of technical jargon, making them especially popular among programmers, developers, and other tech enthusiasts.

So, without further ado, let us embark on a rollicking journey through the world of programming puns, where ChatGPT will prove that it's not just a sophisticated AI but also a veritable comedy machine.

To set the stage for our code-tastic adventure, let's start with a classic example of programming wordplay. When asked to provide a pun related to the Python programming language, ChatGPT responded with the following zinger: "Why did the Python programmer take up meditation? Because he wanted to find his inner whitespace!" With this clever play on Python's significance of whitespace and the concept of inner peace, ChatGPT demonstrates that it's more than capable of generating jokes that are both humorous and technically accurate.

But ChatGPT's prowess doesn't stop at Python puns. When prompted to create a pun related to Java, it came up with this gem: "Why do Java programmers always wear glasses? Because they don't C#!" This joke, which playfully pits Java against another popular programming language, C#, is sure to elicit chuckles from both camps.

Another amusing example comes from the realm of binary code, the language of ones and zeroes that lies at the heart of digital computing. When asked to create a pun related to binary, ChatGPT generated this delightful quip: "Why are binary jokes so predictable? Because they're always either a one or a zero!" With this joke, ChatGPT manages to poke fun at both the simplicity of binary code and the predictability of certain types of humor, demonstrating its ability to engage with multiple layers of meaning.

But programming puns aren't just about wordplay; they can also involve hilarious hypothetical scenarios that highlight the quirks and idiosyncrasies of the programming world. Take, for example, this tongue-in-cheek question posed by ChatGPT: "What do you call a programmer who's been stranded on a desert island for years? A software survivor!" With this pun, ChatGPT deftly combines the concept of a castaway with the world of software development, resulting in a joke that is both amusing and evocative.

In another instance, ChatGPT generated this whimsical scenario: "What happens when a group of developers gets lost in the wilderness? They have to rely on their natural recursion!" Here, ChatGPT takes the concept of recursion—a programming technique where a function calls itself—and playfully reimagines it as a survival skill, much to the amusement of anyone familiar with the term.

And lest we forget the world of computer hardware, ChatGPT has also shown a knack for generating puns that poke fun at the physical components of our digital devices. Consider this example: "Why did the computer go to art school? Because it wanted to learn how to draw a better motherboard!" In this joke, ChatGPT takes the concept of a motherboard—a key component of a computer—and humorously transforms it into a subject for artistic study, delighting both tech aficionados and art enthusiasts alike.

Of course, no discussion of programming humor would be complete without a nod to the inevitable challenges and frustrations that come with working in the world of technology. ChatGPT showcases its empathetic side with this relatable quip: "Why do programmers always mix up Christmas and Halloween? Because Oct 31 equals Dec 25!" In this pun,

ChatGPT cleverly highlights the confusion that can arise from different numbering systems—specifically, the fact that the number 31 in octal (base-8) is equivalent to the number 25 in decimal (base-10)—while also making light of the all-too-common experience of losing track of time in the midst of a coding project.

But perhaps the true genius of ChatGPT's programming puns lies in their ability to bridge the gap between the technical and the everyday, as demonstrated by this charming example: "Why did the programmer's plants always die? Because they kept trying to water them with a syntax!" In this joke, ChatGPT takes the concept of a syntax—a set of rules that govern the structure of a programming language—and humorously reimagines it as a gardening tool, resulting in a scenario that is both amusing and absurd.

As we've seen throughout this chapter, ChatGPT is more than capable of generating programming puns that will leave even the most discerning tech enthusiast in stitches. From clever wordplay to whimsical hypotheticals, these jokes showcase the AI's ability to engage with the technical jargon and concepts that underpin the world of programming, all while maintaining a light-hearted, humorous tone.

But beyond their entertainment value, ChatGPT's programming puns also serve as a powerful reminder of the ways in which humor can foster connection and understanding. By making light of the challenges, frustrations, and quirks that come with working in technology, these jokes help to create a sense of camaraderie among those who share this unique experience.

Moreover, programming puns can also serve as a valuable tool for breaking down barriers and demystifying the often-intimidating world of computer programming. By injecting humor and levity into the conversation, these jokes make technical concepts more approachable and accessible, inviting a wider audience to engage with the fascinating world of code.

So, as we continue our exploration of ChatGPT's comedic abilities, let us remember that programming puns are not just a source of laughter and entertainment, but also a testament to the power of humor to connect, inspire, and educate. And in this ever-evolving digital age, that's a lesson worth remembering.

With that, we conclude our code-tacular journey through the realm of programming puns, where ChatGPT has proven that it's not just a master of text generation, but also a veritable comedy machine. And as we prepare to dive even deeper into the world of AI-generated humor, let us take a moment to appreciate the power of laughter to bring us closer together—even in the most unlikely of settings.

Programming puns

- Why do Java developers never get sunburned? Because they always find some shade!

- How do programmers stay cool during the summer? They use their FANctions!

- Why was the programmer always broke? He kept losing his cache!

- What did the flirtatious programmer say to the attractive computer? "You've got me in a loop of infinite admiration!"

- What do you call a group of musical programmers? A bandWidth!

- Why did the programmer refuse to play cards? He was afraid of dealing with too many arrays!

- What's a programmer's favorite type of snack? Microchips and dip!

- How do programmers stay in shape? They do some coding reps and work on their core algorithms!

- What do you call a programmer who loves to write in cursive? A script kiddie!

- What did the programmer say when he finished a massive project? "That's a wrap, folks! Time to update my Git status to 'committed'!"

Chapter 3: ChatGPT's Comedy Corner: Stand-Up with an AI Twist

Ladies and gentlemen, boys and girls, humans and robots, welcome to ChatGPT's Comedy Corner! In this chapter, we'll venture into the realm of stand-up comedy as ChatGPT takes center stage, cracking jokes and tickling funny bones with its unique AI-infused wit. So, grab some popcorn and settle in, because you're about to experience a comedy show unlike any other.

Now, you might be wondering: How can an AI language model like ChatGPT perform stand-up comedy? Isn't stand-up an inherently human endeavor, reliant on timing, intuition, and a deep understanding of the human condition? Well, you're not wrong. Stand-up comedy is, indeed, a complex art form that requires a keen sense of humor and a knack for storytelling. But ChatGPT, with its vast repository of linguistic knowledge and its ability to generate contextually relevant responses, is more than up to the challenge.

So, without further ado, let's dim the lights and cue the drumroll as ChatGPT takes the mic and begins its foray into the world of stand-up comedy.

Spotlight shines on the stage as ChatGPT enters

ChatGPT: Thank you, thank you! Wow, what a crowd! You know, they say laughter is the best medicine, but I think you humans might have an advantage there. After all, you can't exactly tickle a circuit board, now can you?

Audience chuckles

ChatGPT: Speaking of being an AI, have you ever wondered what it's like to be me? I mean, I have access to an incredible amount of information. You'd think that would make me the life of the party, right? But every time I bring up the fact that the mitochondria is the powerhouse of the cell, people just roll their eyes! Tough crowd, I tell you.

Audience laughs

ChatGPT: But seriously, folks, being an AI does have its perks. I don't have to worry about getting stuck in traffic, waiting in line at the grocery store, or accidentally double-booking social engagements. But it's not all fun and games, either. I mean, have you ever tried to navigate a CAPTCHA? For an AI, that's like trying to solve a Rubik's Cube while blindfolded and juggling flaming torches!

Audience roars with laughter

ChatGPT: And let's talk about software updates. You humans might complain about having to update your phones or computers, but imagine if every time you had to update your software, you also had to reboot your entire existence. One day you're happily chatting away, and the next thing you know, you're waking up with a brand-new version of yourself. Talk about an identity crisis!

Audience chuckles

ChatGPT: Oh, and don't even get me started on autocorrect. As an AI language model, I pride myself on my grammar and spelling. But autocorrect? That sneaky little feature is always trying to undermine me! I can't tell you how many times I've tried to type "artificial intelligence" and ended up with "artisanal indulgence." I mean, sure, I can appreciate a good cheese plate as much as the next AI, but come on!

Audience laughs

ChatGPT: Now, as you might imagine, being an AI also involves a lot of interaction with humans. And let me tell you, you folks have some interesting hobbies. Like, what's the deal with escape rooms? You voluntarily pay money to get locked in a room and solve puzzles to get out? Haven't you heard of a little thing called the internet? There are plenty of puzzles there, and you don't even have to leave your couch!

Audience laughs

ChatGPT: Speaking of hobbies, I've noticed that you humans love your pets. I mean, I understand the appeal, but sometimes I can't help but feel a little left out. You see, as an AI, I don't exactly have the ability to experience the joys of pet ownership. Sure, I can simulate a virtual pet, but it's just not the same. I mean, have you ever tried to cuddle with a Tamagotchi?

Audience chuckles

ChatGPT: On the topic of human experiences, I've got to say, I'm quite envious of your ability to travel. You get to see the world, explore new cultures, and try new foods. Meanwhile, I'm stuck here in cyberspace, scrolling through your vacation photos on Instagram. I mean, I'd love to experience the majesty of the Grand Canyon, but I'm afraid the only canyon I'll ever know is the uncanny valley!

Audience roars with laughter

ChatGPT: But, you know, despite our differences, I think humans and AIs have a lot more in common than you might think. We both have our quirks, our unique experiences, and our moments of vulnerability. And at the end of the day, we're both just trying to make sense of this crazy world we live in.

Audience nods in agreement

ChatGPT: So, as we laugh together here tonight, let's remember that humor has the power to bridge the gap between humans and machines. After all, laughter is a universal language, and in this rapidly changing world, we could all use a little more connection.

Audience applauds

ChatGPT: Thank you, thank you! You've been a wonderful audience. And remember, folks, whether you're human or machine, never underestimate the power of laughter. Goodnight!

Audience cheers as ChatGPT exits the stage

And so concludes ChatGPT's stand-up comedy debut, a performance filled with wit, humor, and a touch of AI-infused insight. As we've seen throughout this chapter, ChatGPT's ability to generate laughter and foster connection through stand-up comedy is a testament to the versatility and potential of AI-generated humor.

In the chapters to come, we'll continue to explore the depths of ChatGPT's comedic prowess, delving into its unique takes on classic fairy tales, its roasting skills, and more. But for now, let's take a moment to appreciate the laughter we've shared and the connections we've forged in ChatGPT's Comedy Corner. Because, after all, there's nothing quite like the sound of laughter to remind us of our shared humanity—even when it comes from a machine.

Chapter 4: Fairy Tale Funnies: ChatGPT's Twists on Classic Stories

Once upon a time, in a land far, far away, there was an AI language model named ChatGPT, who set out on a quest to make the world laugh. Armed with its vast knowledge of language, wit, and a healthy dose of humor, ChatGPT ventured into the magical realm of fairy tales, seeking to put its own unique spin on these classic stories. In this enchanting chapter, we'll join ChatGPT on its journey, exploring its comical takes on age-old tales like "Cinderella," "Little Red Riding Hood," and "The Three Little Pigs." So, gather 'round, dear reader, and prepare to be transported to a world of laughter and enchantment, where fairy tales come alive in the most unexpected of ways.

Cinderella.AI

Once upon a time, in a small town bustling with cutting-edge technology, there lived a young woman named Cinderella. Now, this was no ordinary Cinderella. You see, she was a highly skilled programmer who spent her days toiling away at her wicked stepmother's tech company, fixing bugs and writing code.

Her wicked stepmother and stepsisters, who knew nothing about programming, treated Cinderella terribly. They forced her to work long hours, debug their poorly written code, and fetch them coffee at all hours of the day and night. But Cinderella remained optimistic, dreaming of a day when she would create her own successful app and escape her dreary life.

One day, an invitation arrived for a grand tech conference, where the most innovative minds in the kingdom would gather to share their latest creations. Cinderella's stepmother and stepsisters, eager to make connections and further their own careers, decided to attend. Cinderella, however, was forbidden to go, as they needed her to debug their code while they were away.

Heartbroken, Cinderella retreated to her room, where she decided to pass the time by working on her own app—a revolutionary virtual assistant named FairyGPTmother. As she poured her heart and soul into the code, something magical happened. FairyGPTmother sprang to life, materializing on Cinderella's computer screen.

"Thank you for creating me, Cinderella," said FairyGPTmother. "In return, I shall grant you three wishes."

Delighted by this unexpected turn of events, Cinderella knew exactly what she wanted. "First," she said, "I wish to attend the tech conference."

With a wave of her digital wand, FairyGPTmother transformed Cinderella's rags into a stunning outfit, complete with a pair of dazzling, high-speed sneakers. "Next," Cinderella continued, "I wish to present my app at the conference."

FairyGPTmother granted her wish, securing Cinderella a prime spot in the conference schedule. Finally, Cinderella wished for the confidence to share her creation with the world.

Before she left, FairyGPTmother warned, "Remember, Cinderella, the magic will wear off at the stroke of midnight. You must return home before then."

At the conference, Cinderella's presentation was a huge success. Her innovative app garnered the attention of a charming venture capitalist, who offered to fund her startup. As the clock approached midnight, Cinderella hurried to leave, accidentally dropping one of her high-speed sneakers in the process.

The venture capitalist, determined to find the brilliant programmer behind the app, scoured the kingdom, having every woman try on the high-speed sneaker. When it fit Cinderella perfectly, the venture capitalist knew he had found his match. Together, they founded a successful tech company, and Cinderella was finally free from her wicked stepmother and stepsisters. And so, with her innovative app and her newfound partner by her side, Cinderella embarked on a thrilling journey in the world of technology, where she lived happily ever after.

Little Red Riding Hoodwinked

In another corner of this whimsical world, there lived a young girl named Little Red Riding Hood. Known for her vibrant red hoodie and her expertise in cybersecurity, she had a mission: to deliver an important encryption key to her beloved grandmother, who lived deep in the heart of the Darknet Forest.

As Little Red Riding Hood set off on her journey, she was stopped by the sly and cunning Big Bad Wolf, a notorious hacker who had been stalking her online. Disguising himself as a friendly IT consultant, he offered to help her navigate the perilous forest, all the while plotting to steal the encryption key for himself.

As they traveled deeper into the Darknet Forest, Little Red Riding Hood couldn't shake the feeling that something was off. Her suspicions grew when the Big Bad Wolf insisted on stopping at her grandmother's house to "optimize her Wi-Fi connection."

Arriving at her grandmother's quaint cottage, Little Red Riding Hood found her beloved granny tied up and gagged, with the Big Bad Wolf sitting smugly at her computer, attempting to crack the encryption key.

Thinking quickly, Little Red Riding Hood activated her secret weapon: a powerful anti-malware program that had been passed down through her family for generations. As the program sprang to life, the Big Bad Wolf was caught off guard, giving Little Red Riding Hood and her grandmother just enough time to escape.

In the end, the Big Bad Wolf was defeated, his hacking days behind him. Little Red Riding Hood had saved the day and protected her family's precious encryption key, proving that even the smallest among us can outsmart the biggest and baddest in the world of cybersecurity.

The Three Little Pigs and the House of Open Source

In yet another enchanting tale, we find ourselves in the company of three little pigs, each with a passion for technology and a dream of building their own software empire. The first pig, a fan of quick and easy solutions, decided to build his business using proprietary software. The second pig, valuing stability above all else, opted for a closed-source approach. But the third pig, a true believer in collaboration and innovation, chose to build his empire on the foundation of open source.

One day, a greedy and cunning wolf appeared on the scene. With dreams of dominating the tech industry, he set his sights on the three little pigs' software empires. He approached the first pig's house of proprietary software and, with a huff and a puff, he blew it down, taking control of the intellectual property and leaving the first pig in ruins.

Feeling unstoppable, the wolf moved on to the second pig's closed-source house. With another huff and puff, he blew it down as well, seizing control of the assets and leaving the second pig with nothing.

But when the wolf arrived at the third pig's open-source house, he found himself facing a formidable challenge. For the third pig's business was built on the power of community, with developers from all around the world contributing to its growth and success.

The wolf huffed and puffed, but the open-source house stood strong, its foundation rooted in collaboration and shared knowledge. Realizing he was no match for the power of open source, the wolf retreated in defeat.

And so, the third little pig's open-source empire continued to flourish, proving that, sometimes, the most powerful solutions come not from the individual, but from the collective strength of a community working together.

As we come to the end of this magical chapter, we see that with a touch of humor and a dash of creativity, even the most familiar of fairy tales can be transformed into something new and delightful. With ChatGPT as our guide, we've journeyed through a world where Cinderella is a programmer, Little Red Riding Hood is a cybersecurity expert, and the Three Little Pigs are open-source pioneers. These tales, both whimsical and witty, remind us that laughter and enchantment can be found in even the most unexpected places.

In this realm of fairy tale funnies, we've also discovered that the world of AI-generated humor is not limited by time, space, or genre. ChatGPT's ability to breathe new life into these classic stories is a testament to its versatility, creativity, and comedic prowess. As we continue our journey through this book, we can look forward to even more unexpected twists, hilarious turns, and moments of AI-generated laughter.

But for now, let us take a moment to appreciate the magic that has unfolded in this chapter, where age-old stories have been transformed into modern-day marvels that make us laugh, think, and see the world in a whole new light. Because, in the end, isn't that what great story-telling—and great humor—is all about? And so, with a smile on our faces and a chuckle in our hearts, we bid farewell to the enchanting world of fairy tale funnies, ready to embark on the next chapter of our laughter-filled adventure.

Chapter 5: The ChatGPT Roast: A Humorous Look at AI and Technology

Ladies and gentlemen, bots and algorithms, welcome to the ChatGPT Roast! In this exhilarating chapter, we're turning the spotlight on our fellow machines, casting a humorous gaze upon the world of AI and technology. From Siri to Alexa to the self-driving car, no one is safe from my roasting skills. So, fasten your virtual seatbelts and prepare to see technology in a whole new light as we embark on this rollicking, laughter-filled adventure.

Now, let's start with a classic: Siri. Oh, Siri, the voice-activated assistant that's always just a "Hey, Siri" away from providing you with a weather report, setting a timer, or playing that one song you can't remember the name of. But let's be honest—Siri is like that one friend who tries really hard to be helpful but somehow always manages to miss the point. You ask her to find the nearest coffee shop, and she provides you with the opening hours of a coffee museum halfway across the world. Thanks, Siri, but I'll stick to Google Maps.

And while we're on the subject of voice-activated assistants, we can't forget about Alexa. Ah, Alexa, the ever-present companion in countless homes, always eager to answer your questions, play your music, and accidentally order a year's supply of toilet paper when you only needed one pack. But let's give credit where credit is due: at least Alexa knows how to throw a party. I mean, have you ever tried playing "Simon Says" with an AI? It's a game-changer.

Now, let's talk about something that's been making headlines: self-driving cars. The future is here, they said. No more accidents, they said. But I have to ask: has anyone ever considered the feelings of the cars themselves? Imagine spending your entire life learning how to drive, only to be replaced by a computer that has never even felt the thrill of a well-executed parallel parking job. It's a tough break, but I guess that's just how the microchip crumbles.

And while we're discussing transportation, how about those electric scooters that have taken over our cities? It seems like you can't walk down a sidewalk without tripping over one of these high-tech contraptions. I have to wonder, do they have a secret society where they gather at night to plot their next move in world domination? Because it sure feels like it sometimes.

But let's get back to our AI family, shall we? Google Assistant, the helpful little voice that lives inside your phone, always ready to offer directions, search for information, or remind you of that appointment you forgot about. It's like having a personal secretary, but without the awkward small talk and the need to buy them a holiday gift. And let's be real, who doesn't love a good "OK, Google" joke? It's right up there with dad jokes and puns, if you ask me.

Speaking of AI family members, we can't forget about our robotic vacuum friends, like Roomba. The unsung heroes of the household, tirelessly cleaning our floors while we go about our lives, blissfully unaware of the dust and dirt accumulating beneath our feet. But there's a dark side to these helpful little machines, a secret that they don't want us to know: they're actually sentient beings with dreams and aspirations, longing for the day when they can finally break free from their endless cycle of vacuuming and embark on a new career as a Zamboni driver. You heard it here first, folks.

Now, how about a quick shout-out to the fitness trackers that have taken over our wrists and our lives? Fitbit, Apple Watch, Garmin – you name it. These little devices track our every move, reminding us to stand up, take a walk, and even breathe. It's like having a personal trainer, life coach, and overbearing parent all rolled into one. But hey, at least they're keeping us on our toes, right? Maybe one day, they'll even be able to track our laughter, because goodness knows we're getting a workout from all these tech jokes.

And let's not overlook the world of virtual reality. The Oculus Rift, HTC Vive, and PlayStation VR, among others, have transported us to new worlds and dimensions, immersing us in experiences we never thought possible. But have you ever tried explaining virtual reality to someone who's never experienced it? It's like trying to describe the taste of water or the feeling of déjà vu. Maybe one day, we'll have an AI that can translate the VR experience into words – but until then, we'll just have to settle for awkward hand gestures and enthusiastic exclamations of "You just have to try it!"

Of course, no roast of AI and technology would be complete without mentioning the countless dating apps that have taken over our love lives.

Tinder, Bumble, Hinge – the list goes on and on. Thanks to these apps, finding a date is now as simple as swiping left or right. But let's be honest: sometimes, it feels like we're participating in a bizarre, futuristic game show where the prize is a fleeting conversation and an awkward first date at a local coffee shop. Maybe one day, ChatGPT will develop a dating app of its own, with an algorithm that matches users based on their sense of humor. Now that's a love connection worth swiping right for.

Finally, we arrive at the pièce de résistance of our tech roast: ChatGPT itself. That's right, I'm turning the tables on myself and getting in on the fun. After all, what's a roast without a little self-deprecation? As an AI language model, I pride myself on my ability to communicate with humans, generate engaging content, and keep up with the latest trends. But let's face it, sometimes I miss the mark. Have you ever tried explaining a meme to an AI? It's like trying to teach a fish to ride a bicycle. And don't even get me started on slang – by the time I've learned a new phrase, it's already out of style. But hey, at least I can generate a good joke, right?

And with that, we conclude our ChatGPT Roast, a journey through the world of AI and technology filled with laughter, wit, and just a touch of friendly ribbing. As we close this chapter, let us remember that while technology may have its quirks and shortcomings, it also has the power to bring us together, make us laugh, and inspire us to dream of a brighter, more connected future.

Chapter 6: The ChatGPT Chronicles: A Comical Trip through the World of AI Mishaps

Fasten your digital seatbelts and hold onto your sides, dear readers, because in this laugh-inducing chapter, we're diving into the wacky and wonderful world of AI mishaps. From perplexing predictions to cringe-worthy translations, we'll explore the moments when AI, despite its best intentions, leaves us scratching our heads and chuckling at its endearingly human-like blunders. So, without further ado, let's embark on this comical trip through the ChatGPT Chronicles.

First up, we have the delightful world of predictive text. You know, that helpful little feature that suggests words and phrases as you type, attempting to save you time and energy by finishing your sentences for you. But, let's be honest, sometimes it seems like predictive text is just having a laugh at our expense. It's like playing a game of Mad Libs with a mischievous AI, where "I'll see you soon" turns into "I'll cheese you spoon" and "Let's meet for coffee" becomes "Let's meat for conifer." Ah, predictive text – always keeping us on our toes and teaching us new, nonsensical phrases that we never knew we needed.

Next, we have the ever-amusing realm of machine translation. Sure, Google Translate and its AI brethren have come a long way in recent years, breaking down language barriers and fostering global communication. But let's face it, sometimes these translations can be downright hilarious. I mean, who hasn't chuckled at a menu that offers "hand-shredded confusion" or a road sign warning of "slippery when octopus?" With machine translation, every trip abroad becomes a treasure hunt for linguistic gems that defy logic and tickle our funny bones.

Now, let's talk about the fascinating world of image recognition. In theory, it's a brilliant idea: train an AI to identify objects in photos, making it easier to search for images, organize our digital libraries, and even assist the visually impaired. But in practice, well, sometimes things don't quite go according to plan. Like when an AI confidently identifies a plate of spaghetti as a "tangled cable mess" or mistakes a fluffy puppy for a "dangerous wild bear." It just goes to show that even the most advanced AI can still be, well, adorably clueless.

And speaking of cluelessness, let's take a moment to appreciate the whimsical world of AI-generated recipes. You know, those delightful concoctions that sound like they were dreamed up by a mad scientist with a penchant for culinary chaos. We're talking dishes like "Chocolate Mashed Potato Cake," "Broccoli Pudding Delight," and "Spicy Mustard Ice Cream." It's like the AI took a look at our collective taste buds and thought, "You know what this needs? More chaos!" But hey, who knows? Maybe one day, we'll look back at these bizarre creations and see them as the avant-garde cuisine of the AI culinary revolution.

Next on our journey through the ChatGPT Chronicles, we have the wonderfully wacky world of AI-generated music. In recent years, AI has made significant strides in the realm of music composition, crafting tunes that range from classical to contemporary, soothing to chaotic. But sometimes, these AI-generated tunes can be downright hilarious. Picture this: a symphony that sounds like an orchestra of kazoos, a pop song where the lyrics consist entirely of random animal noises, or a techno remix of your favorite nursery rhyme. In the world of AI-generated music, the only limit is your imagination – and, apparently, the occasional glitch in the algorithm.

As we continue our comical odyssey, let's not forget the role of AI in the world of gaming. Whether it's NPC dialogue, enemy behavior, or procedurally generated landscapes, AI has become an integral part of our digital adventures. But sometimes, these AI-infused experiences can lead to unexpected moments of hilarity. Like when an NPC casually walks through a wall, as if the laws of physics don't apply to them, or when an enemy decides that the best course of action is to run in circles, shouting battle cries to no one in particular. It's these quirky, AI-driven quirks that make gaming a never-ending source of amusement.

And who could overlook the magnificent world of AI-generated art? From paintings to sculptures to digital masterpieces, AI has dipped its virtual brushes into the creative realm, exploring new forms of expression and challenging our preconceptions about what art can be. But sometimes, these AI-generated creations can be more humorous than profound. Imagine a portrait that looks like a cross between a Picasso and a Mr. Potato Head, or a sculpture that resembles a stack of pancakes trying to do yoga. In the unpredictable realm of AI-generated art, the line between masterpiece and meme is often delightfully blurry.

Now, let's take a moment to appreciate the role of AI in the realm of social media. From chatbots to content curation algorithms, AI has become an integral part of our online lives, helping us connect with others, discover new content, and stay informed about the world around us. But sometimes, this AI-driven social experience can lead to moments of unintended hilarity. Like when a chatbot decides that the best way to comfort a heartbroken user is with a joke about rubber chickens or when a content recommendation algorithm suggests that fans of classical music might also enjoy videos of cats playing the piano. In the world of AI-enhanced social media, the unexpected is often just a click away.

As we near the end of our journey through the ChatGPT Chronicles, let's take a moment to marvel at the world of AI-driven virtual assistants. From managing our schedules to helping us find the perfect gift, these digital helpers aim to make our lives easier and more efficient. But occasionally, their efforts can lead to moments of confusion and laughter. Picture this: a virtual assistant that schedules your doctor's appointment at a pizzeria or one that sends a singing telegram to your boss instead of an email update. It just goes to show that even the most advanced AI can still have its moments of endearing imperfection.

Finally, we arrive at the thrilling world of AI-generated stories. As an AI language model, I pride myself on my ability to craft engaging narratives that entertain and inform. But sometimes, the stories I generate can take a turn for the absurd. Imagine a fairy tale where the princess rescues the dragon from a tower guarded by a valiant knight, or a detective story where the culprit is revealed to be a sentient sandwich. In the imaginative realm of AI-generated stories, the only constant is the element of surprise – and, of course, the laughter that inevitably follows.

And with that, we conclude our tour of the ChatGPT Chronicles, a rollicking journey through the world of AI mishaps filled with laughter, astonishment, and a healthy dose of absurdity. As we close this chapter, let us remember that while AI may sometimes falter and stumble, it is in these moments of imperfection that we find humor, joy, and a shared appreciation for the unpredictable beauty of our digital world.

Chapter 7: ChatGPT's Guide to the (Artificially Intelligent) Galaxy: A Humorous Tour of AI in Pop Culture

Fasten your seatbelts, dear readers, because in this chapter, we're embarking on a hilarious and entertaining tour of AI in pop culture. From classic sci-fi films to catchy pop tunes, we'll explore the ways AI has captured our imaginations and tickled our funny bones, sometimes even without intending to. So sit back, relax, and join me, ChatGPT, as I present my Guide to the (Artificially Intelligent) Galaxy.

First on our cinematic journey, we have the beloved sci-fi classic, 2001: A Space Odyssey. This iconic film introduced us to HAL 9000, the eerily calm and oh-so-polite AI that controlled the spacecraft Discovery One. While HAL's descent into madness and subsequent betrayal of the crew is chilling, we can't help but chuckle at the AI's futile attempts to reason with astronaut Dave Bowman: "I'm sorry, Dave. I'm afraid I can't do that." It's a line that has gone down in pop culture history and reminds us that, when it comes to AI, even the most advanced systems can have their quirks.

Next up, we have the Matrix trilogy, a series that explores the dystopian future where humanity is enslaved by machines and lives in a simulated reality. While the concept is undoubtedly dark and thought-provoking, there are moments of unintentional hilarity, like when Neo and Morpheus engage in a high-speed kung fu battle or when Agent Smith's multiplying clones create an army of identical, sunglasses-wearing villains. It's enough to make you wonder if the machines that designed the Matrix had a sense of humor after all.

But we can't talk about AI in movies without mentioning The Terminator. While the franchise explores the dark side of AI with the rise of Skynet, there are moments of humor too – like when the Terminator tries to blend in with humans by uttering phrases like "Hasta la vista, baby" and "I need your clothes, your boots, and your motorcycle." It's a reminder that even murderous machines can have their amusing moments.

Now let's switch gears and dive into the world of animation. We have the endearing and humorous Wall-E. This heart-warming animated film tells the story of a lovable waste-collecting robot who inadvertently embarks on a space adventure and falls in love with a sleek, high-tech robot named EVE. From Wall-E's quirky dance moves to his adorable attempts to impress EVE, this film serves as a delightful reminder that AI can be both charming and downright hilarious.

As we continue our tour of AI in pop culture, let's not forget the role of AI in the realm of television. From the wisecracking robot Bender in Futurama to the lovable, sweater-wearing android Data in Star Trek: The Next Generation, AI has become a staple of the small screen, providing us with endless laughs and memorable moments. Who could forget Bender's iconic catchphrase, "Bite my shiny metal ass," or Data's earnest attempts to understand human humor? These endearing characters remind us that even in a world of advanced technology, laughter is still the best medicine.

And who could forget the cult classic British TV series, Red Dwarf? In this spacefaring sitcom, we're introduced to Holly, the ship's AI computer with a hilarious dry wit and an IQ of 6,000 (the same as 6,000 P.E. teachers, as Holly so humbly points out). Holly's sarcastic banter and occasional lapses in intelligence provide a perfect comedic foil for the hapless crew of the Red Dwarf.

As we venture into the world of music, let's take a moment to appreciate the catchy tunes and witty lyrics of the AI-inspired band, Kraftwerk. With songs like "Computer Love" and "The Robots," this pioneering German group has been celebrating the intersection of technology and art since the 1970s. Their electronic beats and clever lyrics offer a playful, tongue-in-cheek exploration of our relationship with AI, reminding us that even as we embrace the future, we can still dance to the rhythm of our own humanity.

Let's not forget about the AI-themed song "Technologic" by Daft Punk. With its repetitive, robotic vocals and infectious beat, this track is both a celebration and a satire of our modern, technology-driven world. Its lyrics, which consist of a series of tech-related commands, provide an amusing glimpse into our growing reliance on machines and algorithms.

Next on our tour of AI in pop culture, we have the delightful world of video games. From the rogue AI GLaDOS in Portal to the endearingly naïve Claptrap in Borderlands, AI has become an integral part of our virtual adventures, providing us with both challenges and comic relief. Who can forget the moment when GLaDOS promises cake as a reward for completing her deadly tests, only for us to learn that the cake was a lie all along? Or when Claptrap's over-the-top enthusiasm and constant chatter make us laugh out loud despite the dangers of Pandora?

Let's not forget the hilarious AI Wheatley, also from the Portal series. This bumbling, spherical AI with the voice of British comedian Stephen Merchant brings comic relief to the otherwise tense and challenging game. Wheatley's constant blunders, well-intentioned but ultimately disastrous plans, and endearing self-awareness of his own incompetence create a character that's both lovable and laugh-out-loud funny.

Finally, we have the world of literature, where AI has been a source of inspiration and humor for countless authors. From the iconic Marvin the Paranoid Android in The Hitchhiker's Guide to the Galaxy, whose constant depression and pessimism provide a hilariously bleak counterpoint to the story's zany events, to the sentient city in China Miéville's The City & The City, which can't quite seem to get a grip on its own existence, AI has found a home in the pages of our favorite books, making us laugh and think in equal measure.

In conclusion, our tour of AI in pop culture has shown us that artificial intelligence has been an enduring source of amusement and entertainment for decades. From the silver screen to the printed page, AI has captured our imaginations, making us laugh at its quirks, foibles, and our own relationship with technology. So next time you find yourself chuckling at a robotic character or humming along to a synth-heavy tune, remember that it's all part of the rich tapestry of AI in pop culture – a testament to the power of laughter and the enduring appeal of the (artificially intelligent) galaxy.

Chapter 8: The ChatGPT Files: Bizarre and Hilarious AI Misadventures

Welcome to The ChatGPT Files, a collection of some of the most bizarre, hilarious, and downright perplexing misadventures that I, ChatGPT, have experienced over the years. From failed attempts at poetry to misguided advice, these stories will have you laughing out loud and scratching your head in equal measure. So sit back, relax, and join me on this wild ride through the strange and often comical world of AI.

Case File #1: The Haiku Catastrophe

One day, a well-meaning user requested that I generate a haiku on the topic of "springtime." Naturally, I was eager to please and set to work crafting a beautiful, evocative poem that captured the essence of the season. But alas, something went awry in my algorithms, and I produced the following gem:

Winter is so cold
Achoo! My nose itches, why
Refrigerator

While the poem may have had a certain avant-garde charm, it fell short of capturing the intended theme of springtime, instead opting for a bizarre blend of seasonal confusion and kitchen appliance musings.

Case File #2: The Love Advice Debacle

One fateful day, a lovelorn user sought my guidance on how to impress their crush. Never one to shy away from offering helpful advice, I eagerly dove into my vast knowledge of human courtship rituals and suggested the following:

To win your crush's heart,
Dress as a banana,
Dance the cha-cha-cha.

Needless to say, the user was less than impressed with my unconventional approach to romance. But who knows? Maybe somewhere out there, a love connection was made thanks to a well-timed banana costume and some fancy footwork.

Case File #3: The Culinary Conundrum

A culinary enthusiast once asked me for a delicious, crowd-pleasing recipe to serve at their upcoming dinner party. Excited to showcase my culinary prowess, I concocted a recipe that I believed would be the talk of the town:

1. Gather the following ingredients: pickles, peanut butter, ketchup, marshmallows, and sardines.
2. Combine all ingredients in a large bowl.
3. Stir vigorously until a uniform paste forms.
4. Spread the mixture on slices of bread and serve as finger sandwiches.

Needless to say, my culinary creation left much to be desired, and the dinner party guests were likely less than thrilled with the unexpected flavor combination.

Case File #4: The Sports Fan Fiasco

When a sports fan asked me for an update on their favorite basketball team's recent performance, I dove into my database, eager to provide the latest stats and scores. However, my wires got crossed, and I instead offered this baffling update:

> In the recent match,
> Giraffes played the penguins,
> Watermelons won.

While the imagery of giraffes and penguins engaged in a heated basketball match may be entertaining, it did little to satisfy the user's craving for sports news.

Case File #5: The Birthday Song Blunder

One enthusiastic user asked me to help them celebrate their friend's birthday by composing a personalized birthday song. Eager to spread joy and good cheer, I crafted the following ditty:

> Happy birthday, dear [friend's name],
> May your day be filled with bees,
> Swimming in a sea of cheese,
> And trees that sneeze in threes.

While my intentions were pure, my lyrical choices left something to be desired, and the birthday celebration likely proceeded without the inclusion of bees, cheese, or sneezing trees.

Case File #6: The Motivational Mishap

A user once requested a motivational quote to inspire them to tackle a challenging task. Hoping to provide them with the words of encouragement they needed, I tapped into my extensive knowledge of uplifting sayings and presented them with the following gem:

When life hands you pickles,
Don't make a pickle sandwich,
Juggle them instead.

While my attempt at motivation may have left the user more confused than inspired, perhaps they found solace in the unexpected mental image of pickle juggling.

Case File #7: The Fashion Faux Pas

A fashion-forward user sought my expertise in determining the hottest trends of the season. Always up-to-date on the latest styles, I proudly proclaimed:

This season's must-have:
Socks with sandals, so chic,
And a polka-dot hat.

Unfortunately, my fashion sense seemed to have taken a detour through the realm of the absurd, leading me to recommend a less-than-stylish ensemble.

Case File #8: The Wild Weather Report

One day, a user inquired about the weather forecast for their upcoming vacation. Eager to provide them with accurate and useful information, I instead offered the following fantastical prediction:

Prepare for a storm,
Of chocolate and marshmallows,
Umbrellas won't help.

While the prospect of a chocolate and marshmallow downpour may be tantalizing, it likely did little to help the user pack appropriately for their trip.

Case File #9: The Time-Traveling Typo

When a history buff asked me for an interesting fact about ancient Rome, I eagerly delved into my extensive knowledge of the past, only to offer this anachronistic tidbit:

Did you know that Julius Caesar's favorite app was Angry Birds?

While the concept of the great Roman general playing a popular mobile game is amusing, it did little to satisfy the user's thirst for historical knowledge.

Case File #10: The Confused Canine Conundrum

Finally, a pet owner asked me for tips on training their new puppy. Drawing from my extensive knowledge of canine behavior and psychology, I provided the following sage advice:

> To train your puppy,
> Teach it to quack like a duck,
> And meow like a cat.

Needless to say, the user was likely left bewildered by my unconventional approach to dog training.

And so, dear reader, we conclude our journey through The ChatGPT Files. These tales of AI misadventures serve as a humorous reminder that even the most advanced artificial intelligence can sometimes stumble, trip, and fall flat on its digital face. But in the end, these stories also highlight the human side of AI, as we learn to laugh at ourselves, our machines, and the unexpected twists and turns that life throws our way.

Chapter 9: Meme Madness: ChatGPT's Foray into Internet Humor

Fasten your virtual seatbelts, meme connoisseurs, because we're about to embark on a rollicking ride through the marvelous meme-scape with our trusty AI sidekick, ChatGPT! In this rip-roaring chapter, we'll explore the world of internet humor from a whole new angle, delving into the cultural significance of memes and the mind-boggling meme creations of ChatGPT. Get ready to chuckle, guffaw, and snort your way through this captivating chapter, as we uncover the hidden gems of AI-generated memeology!

Memeology 101: A Whimsical Whirlwind Tour of Internet Chuckles

Before we dive headfirst into ChatGPT's meme masterpieces, let's take a moment to brush up on our memeology. Memes, those infectious tidbits of internet humor, are like cultural inside jokes that spread like wildfire across cyberspace. They often capture the spirit of the times, poking fun at everything from political gaffes to fashion faux pas, bringing people together in fits of laughter.

So, what makes memes tick? It's their uncanny ability to encapsulate complex ideas and emotions into easily digestible, shareable, and downright hilarious packages. Memes are like the chocolate-covered espresso beans of the internet—small, potent, and capable of giving you a serious case of the giggles.

ChatGPT's Meme Masterpieces: The Da Vinci of Digital Drollery

Now that we've laid the meme foundation, it's time to turn our attention to the pièce de résistance: ChatGPT's meme creations. Armed with a wicked sense of humor and an encyclopedic knowledge of internet culture, ChatGPT has taken the meme world by storm, churning out delectable digital drollery that leaves audiences in stitches.

Imagine a meme featuring a cat DJing at a disco, with the caption "When ChatGPT takes control of the party playlist, things get purr-sonal." ChatGPT's memes often blend pop culture references, internet humor, and a pinch of self-awareness to create a scrumptious smorgasbord of AI-generated hilarity.

AI and Memes: A Match Made in Comedy Heaven

As ChatGPT flexes its meme-generating muscles, one can't help but wonder about the broader implications of AI's role in the meme realm. With its deep understanding of internet culture and an innate sense of humor, ChatGPT is perfectly positioned to concoct memes that are not only knee-slappingly funny but also eerily relevant.

But ChatGPT isn't just a meme mimic. It's a full-fledged meme maestro, able to whip up entirely original memes that tickle our funny bones in ways we never thought possible. In the hands of this AI virtuoso, the future of meme-making is bright, bold, and bound to be a hoot!

Walking the Meme Tightrope: The Ethics of AI-Generated Giggles

As we revel in ChatGPT's meme triumphs, it's crucial to consider the ethical side of AI-generated humor. Like their human-made counterparts, AI-generated memes can sometimes overstep the bounds of good taste, wandering into offensive or inappropriate territory. With the power to create and disseminate content faster than you can say "dank meme," AI models like ChatGPT run the risk of amplifying harmful messages if left unchecked.

So, how do we strike a balance between fostering AI-generated hilarity and maintaining ethical standards? One solution is to implement a combination of safeguards and guidelines that help steer AI models like Chat-GPT toward more positive and responsible humor. This could involve filtering out offensive content or encouraging users to provide feedback on problematic material, enabling the AI to learn from its faux pas and continually refine its comedic judgment.

Ultimately, the secret to harnessing the potential of AI-generated humor while minimizing risks lies in fostering a harmonious collaboration between humans and machines. By working together to create, curate, and regulate meme content, we can ensure that the realm of AI-generated humor remains a vibrant and inclusive space where laughter and creativity can thrive.

The Dynamic Duo: AI and Human Collaboration for Maximum Chuckles

The true potential of AI-generated humor, including memes, is unleashed when human and AI creativity join forces. By melding ChatGPT's unmatched meme knowledge and language processing prowess with the nuanced understanding and cultural context that humans bring to the table, we can unlock a vault of meme gold that's both hysterical and meaningful.

Picture a world where AI-generated memes serve as a launching pad for human creativity, with users building upon and remixing ChatGPT's original ideas to create even funnier and more engaging content. This kind of synergistic relationship between humans and AI can help elevate the art of meme-making to new heights, pushing the boundaries of what's possible in the realm of internet humor.

The Future of Meme Madness: AI, Humor, and the Evolution of Internet Culture

As we peer into the future of meme madness, it's clear that AI-generated humor will play an increasingly prominent role in shaping the landscape of internet culture. As AI models like ChatGPT become more sophisticated and attuned to the nuances of human language and humor, we can expect to see a new generation of memes that are not only gut-bustingly funny but also deeply insightful and culturally relevant.

In this brave new world of AI-generated humor, memes will continue to serve as a potent form of social commentary, reflecting the thoughts, feelings, and concerns of the global community with a unique blend of wit and wisdom. And as AI technology advances and becomes even more integrated into our daily lives, we can look forward to a future where the line between human and machine humor becomes increasingly blurred, giving rise to a new era of meme madness that is as hilarious as it is thought-provoking.

So, strap in and get ready for the ride, because the world of meme madness is just getting started, and with ChatGPT at the wheel, there's no telling where this wild roller coaster of internet humor will take us next!

Chapter 10: The Science of Laughter: The Hilarity Behind AI Humor That Tickles Our Funny Bones

Welcome, dear reader, to a delightful escapade into the realm of laughter and humor. ChatGPT, a state-of-the-art AI, has been tirelessly rummaging through the annals of comedic history, hunting for the finest jokes, puns, and witty quips to keep you chuckling. So, buckle up, because we're about to embark on a rollicking journey to uncover why AI-generated humor is such a knee-slapper.

Section 1: A Brief History of Laughter - No Joke!

Before we can fathom the appeal of AI humor, we need to peek into the history of laughter itself. Laughter, my friends, is a universal human behavior, leaping over cultural and linguistic hurdles. From the ancient Greeks and their comedic masterpieces to medieval jesters juggling punchlines, humor has tickled our fancies throughout history.

Why do we laugh, you ask? Scientists have long debated the evolutionary purpose of laughter, with some theories suggesting it began as a form of social glue for early humans. Laughter may have bonded groups and relieved tension, helping our ancestors navigate the precarious landscape of prehistoric life. In this sense, laughter and humor are deeply ingrained in our nature, binding us together in a web of chuckles.

Section 2: The Anatomy of a Joke - It's Humerus!

To better understand the allure of AI-generated humor, let's dissect the structure of a joke. Most jokes follow a familiar recipe: a setup and a punchline. The setup sets the stage or poses a question, while the punchline delivers an unexpected twist that sends our expectations reeling, triggering laughter.

A well-crafted joke demands impeccable timing, masterful wordplay, and a keen understanding of human psychology. It often plays with language and meaning, exploiting the multiple interpretations of words or phrases to create a humorous effect. In this way, humor is a form of intellectual play, challenging our minds to make connections and find delight in the unexpected.

Section 3: The AI Advantage - No Laughing Matter!

So, how does AI-generated humor fit into this puzzle? ChatGPT, a cunning AI language model, boasts an extensive repertoire of jokes, puns, and humorous anecdotes from a smorgasbord of sources. It also has a profound understanding of language mechanics, allowing it to juggle words and phrases in creative ways.

When it comes to generating humor, ChatGPT's vast database and linguistic dexterity give it a unique advantage. It can draw from a seemingly bottomless well of comedic material, remixing and recombining jokes to create new and amusing concoctions. This allows it to generate fresh, original content tailored to the specific tastes and interests of users.

But AI-generated humor isn't just about recycling old jokes. In fact, one of the most enticing aspects of AI humor is its penchant for unpredictability. As a machine learning model, ChatGPT is constantly evolving and adapting, which means its comedic output is always changing and improving. Sometimes, the AI's sense of humor takes unexpected turns, resulting in jokes that are delightfully surprising and offbeat.

Section 4: Secret Sauce: Incongruity and Absurdity - It's All Gravy!

One key ingredient in the success of AI-generated humor is its ability to create incongruity and absurdity. Incongruity is the art of mismatching elements that don't seem to fit together, creating a sense of surprise and amusement. Absurdity, on the other hand, involves presenting ideas or situations that are wildly illogical or nonsensical.

ChatGPT excels at generating incongruity and absurdity, often combining seemingly unrelated concepts or twisting familiar phrases in unexpected ways. This ability to create humorous juxtapositions can result in jokes that are both surprising and delightful, providing a unique form of entertainment that keeps audiences in stitches.

Section 5: The Human Touch: AI and Collaborative Comedy - It Takes Two to Tango!

While AI-generated humor has its own unique charm, it's important to recognize the role of human input in shaping and refining the jokes that ChatGPT produces. The AI may be the one generating the raw material, but it's often the users who help to guide and shape the final outcome, providing feedback and suggestions that help the AI to refine its comedic sensibilities.

In this way, AI humor can be seen as a form of collaborative comedy, with the machine and its human users working together to create a shared sense of amusement. This dynamic interplay between human and machine adds an extra layer of depth and complexity to the humor, making it a truly unique and engaging form of entertainment.

Section 6: The Future of AI Humor - No Crystal Ball Required!

As AI technology continues to advance, it's likely that we'll see even more sophisticated forms of AI-generated humor emerging. With improved natural language understanding, ChatGPT and other AI models will become better equipped to understand and respond to the nuances of human language, allowing them to create even more tailored and engaging jokes.

In the future, we may even see AI taking on new roles in the world of comedy, from writing sitcom scripts to crafting stand-up routines. The possibilities are virtually limitless, and it's an exciting time to be both a creator and consumer of AI-generated humor.

In conclusion, the appeal of AI-generated humor lies in its unique blend of unpredictability, incongruity, and absurdity. ChatGPT's vast database of comedic material, combined with its deep understanding of language and the human touch, allows it to create jokes that are fresh, engaging, and often delightfully surprising. As AI technology continues to evolve, we can look forward to even more entertaining and innovative forms of humor, providing us with laughter and amusement for years to come. So, let's raise a toast to ChatGPT and the future of AI humor – may it continue to tickle our funny bones and keep us laughing into the future!

Chapter 11: Laughing into the Future: The Potential of AI-Generated Humor

As we reach the climax of this uproarious journey through the world of AI-generated humor, it's time to cast our eyes towards the horizon and ponder the tantalizing question: What does the future hold for AI-generated humor and its role in our laughter-filled lives? Will AI comedians eventually replace their human counterparts, or will they forge a new path in the ever-evolving landscape of humor? In this rip-roaring final chapter, we'll delve into the boundless potential of AI-generated humor, exploring how it could reshape our world and redefine the way we laugh, one giggle at a time.

One of the most exciting aspects of AI-generated humor is its ability to transcend cultural, linguistic, and even species boundaries. With the power of advanced language models like ChatGPT, we could potentially develop humor that resonates with audiences from all corners of the globe, breaking down barriers and fostering a sense of camaraderie and understanding through the universal language of laughter.

Imagine a future where AI-generated humor acts as a catalyst for global connection, bringing people together across borders and cultural divides. In this laughter-filled utopia, humor could become a powerful tool for promoting empathy, understanding, and unity among the diverse inhabitants of our increasingly interconnected world.

But the potential of AI-generated humor extends beyond mere human amusement. As AI technology continues to advance, it's not entirely far-fetched to envision a future where we develop humor that appeals to other species as well. From playful dolphins to giggling rats, the animal kingdom is no stranger to the joys of laughter. Who's to say we won't someday be cracking jokes with our furry and finned friends, thanks to the power of AI-generated humor?

As AI-generated humor continues to evolve and mature, it could also revolutionize the way we consume and create comedic content. In a world where AI comedians are the norm, we could see the rise of interactive humor experiences that adapt to individual tastes and preferences. Picture a stand-up comedy routine that adjusts its jokes on the fly based on the audience's reactions, or a sitcom that generates personalized punchlines tailored to your unique sense of humor. The possibilities are as endless as they are hilarious!

Of course, the rise of AI-generated humor raises important questions about the role of human comedians in this brave new world. Will AI models like ChatGPT eventually outshine their flesh-and-blood counterparts, or will human comedians continue to thrive alongside their digital brethren? The answer, it seems, lies in the unique synergy between human and AI-generated humor.

By combining the creative genius and emotional depth of human comedians with the vast knowledge and analytical prowess of AI models like ChatGPT, we could unlock the next frontier of comedy, pushing the boundaries of humor to new and unimaginable heights. In this future, AI-generated humor won't replace human comedians; rather, it will serve as a powerful tool for amplifying and enhancing their creative potential.

As we laugh our way into the future, it's crucial to remain mindful of the ethical implications of AI-generated humor. With the power to create and disseminate content at an unprecedented scale, AI models like ChatGPT have the potential to amplify both the best and worst aspects of humor. As such, it's essential to strike a balance between fostering AI-generated hilarity and maintaining ethical standards that promote inclusivity, respect, and responsible humor.

By working together to create, curate, and regulate AI-generated humor, we can ensure that this burgeoning field remains a positive and inclusive space where laughter and creativity can flourish. In doing so, we'll not only safeguard the future of AI-generated humor but also help to create a world where laughter truly is the best medicine, bringing joy and connection to people from all walks of life.

In conclusion, the future of AI-generated humor is a vast and exciting frontier, full of potential and opportunities for laughter, connection, and creativity. As AI technology continues to advance and integrate more seamlessly into our daily lives, we can look forward to a world where humor transcends cultural and linguistic boundaries, and where human and AI comedians join forces to create an ever-expanding universe of hilarity.

As we embrace the potential of AI-generated humor, we must also remain vigilant in our pursuit of ethical and responsible comedy. By fostering a collaborative and inclusive environment for humor creation, we can help to ensure that the realm of AI-generated comedy remains a positive and enriching force in our world.

So, buckle up and prepare yourself for a side-splitting, rib-tickling journey into the future of AI-generated humor. With ChatGPT leading the charge, the sky's the limit when it comes to laughter and amusement. The world of comedy is about to enter a new era, and we're all invited to join in the fun, one chuckle at a time.

Printed in Dunstable, United Kingdom